T0413820

MILITARY CAREERS

# JOBS IN THE
# MARINE CORPS

by Sloane Hughes

BEARPORT
PUBLISHING

Minneapolis, Minnesota

**Credits**

Cover, © Lance Cpl. Leslie Alcaraz/U. S. Marine Corps, © guvendemir/iStock, © Extarz/Shutterstock, and © P__L__photography/iStock; 5, © Lance Cpl. Bethany Barnoski/DVIDS; 7, © IanDagnall Computing/Alamy Stock Photo; 9T, © Lance Cpl. Juan Bustos/DVIDS; 9B, © Lance Cpl. Angelica Annastas/DVIDS; 10, © U. S. Marine Corps/Wikimedia Commons; 11T, © Lance Cpl. Ethan Miller/DVIDS; 11B, © Staff Sgt. Warren Wright/DVIDS; 13, © Lance Cpl. Andrew Bray/DVIDS; 14–15, © Cpl. Scott Aubuchon/DVIDS; 17T, © Member: 1149277/DVIDS; 17B, © Lance Cpl. Alexis Betances/DVIDS; 19, © Sgt. David Bickel/DVIDS; 21, © Sgt. Sean Potter/DVIDS; 23T, © Cpl. Christian Garcia/DVIDS; 23B, © Lance Cpl. John Hall/DVIDS; 25, © LCpl Tyler S. Dietrich/Wikimedia Commons; 26–27, © Courtesy Photo/DVIDS; 28T, © U.S. Government/Wikimedia Commons; 28B, © Adrian R. Rowan/Wikimedia Commons; 29, © Cpl. Alfred V. Lopez/Wikimedia Commons.

**Bearport Publishing Company Product Development Team**

President: Jen Jenson; Director of Product Development: Spencer Brinker; Managing Editor: Allison Juda; Associate Editor: Naomi Reich; Associate Editor: Tiana Tran; Art Director: Colin O'Dea; Designer: Kim Jones; Designer: Kayla Eggert; Product Development Assistant: Owen Hamlin

**Statement on Usage of Generative Artificial Intelligence**

Bearport Publishing remains committed to publishing high-quality nonfiction books. Therefore, we restrict the use of generative AI to ensure accuracy of all text and visual components pertaining to a book's subject. See BearportPublishing.com for details.

*Library of Congress Cataloging-in-Publication Data*

Title: Jobs in the Marine Corps / by Sloane Hughes.
Description: Minneapolis, Minnesota : Bearport Publishing Company, [2025] |
   Series: Military careers | Includes bibliographical references and
   index.
Identifiers: LCCN 2024010950 (print) | LCCN 2024010951 (ebook) | ISBN
   9798892320382 (library binding) | ISBN 9798892321716 (ebook)
Subjects: LCSH: United States. Marine Corps--Vocational guidance--Juvenile
   literature. | Marines--United States--Juvenile literature.
Classification: LCC VE23 .H75 2025  (print) | LCC VE23  (ebook) | DDC
   359.9/602373--dc23/eng/20240326
LC record available at https://lccn.loc.gov/2024010950
LC ebook record available at https://lccn.loc.gov/2024010951

For more information, write to Bearport Publishing, 5357 Penn Avenue South, Minneapolis, MN 55419.

# CONTENTS

Unlocking Languages . . . . . . . . . . . . . . . . . . . .4

The First Marines . . . . . . . . . . . . . . . . . . . . . .6

Becoming a Marine . . . . . . . . . . . . . . . . . . . . .8

Taking Charge . . . . . . . . . . . . . . . . . . . . . . .12

Battle Ready . . . . . . . . . . . . . . . . . . . . . . . .14

Information Gatherers . . . . . . . . . . . . . . . . . .16

Helping Hands . . . . . . . . . . . . . . . . . . . . . . .18

Not for the Faint of Heart . . . . . . . . . . . . . . .22

Taking Care of Their Own . . . . . . . . . . . . . . .24

Reaching Out . . . . . . . . . . . . . . . . . . . . . . . .26

More about the Marine Corps . . . . . . . . . . . .28

Glossary. . . . . . . . . . . . . . . . . . . . . . . . . . . . 30

Read More. . . . . . . . . . . . . . . . . . . . . . . . . . . 31

Learn More Online. . . . . . . . . . . . . . . . . . . . . 31

Index. . . . . . . . . . . . . . . . . . . . . . . . . . . . . . . 32

About the Author . . . . . . . . . . . . . . . . . . . . .32

# UNLOCKING LANGUAGES

The room is quiet as U.S. Marines tune into their headsets, listening to conversations from around the world. They **transcribe** and **analyze** recordings in other languages, hoping to find clues about what our enemies are possibly planning.

The information a cryptologic language analyst finds may help the military plan **missions** to keep the United States and its people safe. This is just one of the many important jobs in the United States Marine Corps.

---

**CAREER SPOTLIGHT: Cryptologic Language Analyst**

**Job Requirements:**
- At least 17 years old
- Language training
- Enlisted

**Skills and Training:**

 Foreign Languages

 Analyze & Report

 Preventative Maintenance

# THE FIRST MARINES

The first group of marines in the United States was known as the Continental Marines. They formed in 1775, working alongside the United States Navy. During the Revolutionary War (1775–1783), the Continental Marines fought on land and at sea. After the war, both the navy and the marines were broken up.

Years later, the United States needed a military force at sea due to conflicts with pirates. In 1798, Congress reestablished the marines as a new organization—the United States Marine Corps. Today, the marines have both **amphibious** and ground crews ready to protect our country.

★ ★ ★ ★ ★ ★ ★ ★ ★ ★ ★ ★ ★

The marines are often the first branch of the United States military to head into battle. They have been in every war the United States has taken part in.

# BECOMING A MARINE

All **enlisted** marines must pass **recruit** training, or boot camp, before they become full marines. These 13 weeks of intense training teach recruits about military operations and develop their physical and mental strength.

Most of the training focuses on building **combat** and survival skills. Recruits practice with weapons and learn **martial arts**. They face many different drills to prepare for battle, such as crawling on the ground, throwing grenades, and running while carrying another recruit.

★ ★ ★ ★ ★ ★ ★ ★ ★ ★ ★ ★ ★ ★

Each recruit receives a bag of items to help them through training. It includes a waterbottle, sleeping gear, binoculars, a flashlight, and first-aid supplies.

Recruits gain strength through physical drills, such as lifting heavy weights over their heads.

At the end of basic training, the final exercise is called the Crucible. Recruits are divided into groups to complete 8 **simulated** combat experiences for 54 hours. They must face these challenges with little food and sleep.

During one simulation, recruits work together to carry an injured teammate back to safety. Other simulated events include crawling through barbed wire, sneaking behind enemy lines at night, and hiking 48 miles (77 km). After completing the Crucible, recruits are ready to join the United States Marine Corps.

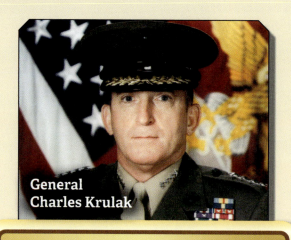

General
Charles Krulak

★ ★ ★ ★ ★ ★ ★ ★ ★ ★ ★ ★

The Crucible was thought up by General Charles Krulak in 1996. The exercise recreates actual combat events from marine corps history.

# TAKING CHARGE

Some marines may become **infantry** riflemen. These marines are the first ones on the front lines, helping the military in many different ways. First, they scout an area to gain knowledge on the enemy, such as where they are located. Whatever information the infantry riflemen find may help them plan attacks. Then, they lead the battle, closing in on the enemy and engaging in close combat. Infantry riflemen also work on the defensive, helping with security patrol.

CAREER SPOTLIGHT: **Infantry Rifleman**

**Job Requirements:**
- At least 17 years old
- 15 weeks infantry training
- Enlisted

**Skills and Training:**
- Offense & Defense
- Weapons Operation
- Physical & Mental Strength

Marines must know how to properly use and maintain rifles.

# BATTLE READY

A fire team leader is in charge of the most basic unit of marine infantry. They tell the other soldiers in the group where to go and who to fire at in combat. The fire team leader helps soldiers stay together if they need to quickly move to take cover from enemy fire.

If the fire team leader gets hurt during battle, the automatic rifleman takes over the lead and tells the other team members what to do. Automatic riflemen are usually in charge of firing weapons against enemy troops of four or more.

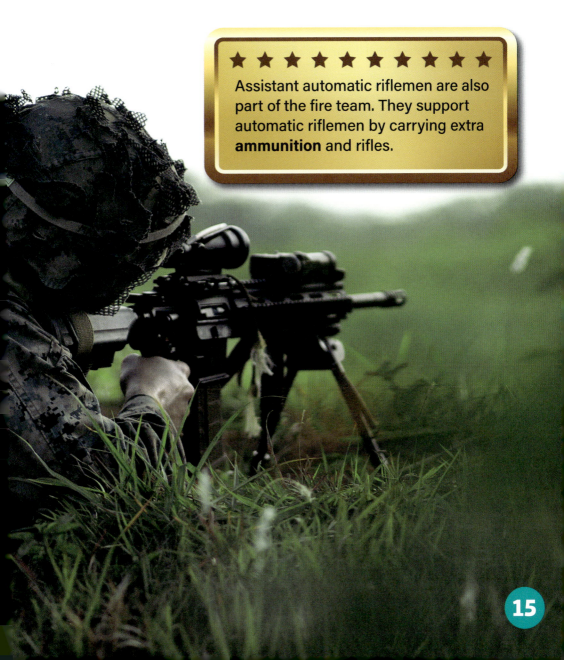

★ ★ ★ ★ ★ ★ ★ ★ ★ ★ ★ ★

Assistant automatic riflemen are also part of the fire team. They support automatic riflemen by carrying extra **ammunition** and rifles.

# INFORMATION GATHERERS

Some marines are information gatherers. Light armored **reconnaissance** marines use **surveillance** skills to determine the location of the enemy. These marines may sometimes go into battle. Light armored reconnaissance marines drive soldiers around in armored vehicles so they can fire at the opposition.

In contrast, reconnaissance marines almost always head directly into enemy territory. These soldiers parachute from helicopters. They then search the area, gather information on the enemy, and pass along whatever they find to the base.

## CAREER SPOTLIGHT: Light Armored Reconnaissance Marine

**Job Requirements:**
- Entry-level
- 6 weeks training
- Enlisted

**Skills and Training:**
- Armored Security
- Reconnaissance & Surveillance
- Weapons Operation

Light armored reconnaissance marines drive special vehicles that can be used in any weather and on all types of land.

A reconnaissance marine parachuting

# HELPING HANDS

Pilots get marines and supplies from one place to another. They take soldiers into and out of battle zones. When the ground forces need extra power, pilots join the fight by attacking enemy aircraft from the skies. They may also disrupt communication signals so the enemy can't call for help.

Airborne and air delivery specialists help with supply drops, too. They pack the items and secure them to pallets so they can be delivered by parachute.

## CAREER SPOTLIGHT: Airborne and Air Delivery Specialist

**Job Requirements:**
- At least 17 years old
- High school diploma or GED
- Enlisted

**Skills and Training:**
- Airborne Operation
- Parachute Packing
- Equipment Recovery

Aircraft are always coming and going from bases. Aviation operations specialists keep track of every aircraft's departure and return, making sure missions stay on time. The specialists also help pilots plan their flight paths. The information on flight times and plans gets passed along to air traffic controllers, who make sure aircraft can take off and land safely. These marines usually work inside towers, where they have a clear view of the runway in order to help guide pilots in flight.

CAREER SPOTLIGHT: **Aviation Operations Specialist**

**Job Requirements:**

- 17 to 28 years old
- 13 weeks training
- Enlisted

**Skills and Training:**

- Aircraft Procedures
- Routes & Navigation
- Communication Systems

Air traffic controllers are
constantly on watch.

# NOT FOR THE FAINT OF HEART

**Explosive** ordnance disposal specialists locate, analyze, and **neutralize** explosive weapons before they go off. First, they identify an explosive, such as a bomb or a mine. Then, these specialists safely take it apart and dispose of the pieces.

K-9 marines are military dogs that can help find explosives, too. Dog handlers work with these animals as they sniff out danger. The handlers train the dogs to find hidden ammunitions as well as illegal drugs. Some handlers work with dogs to find people who are missing or in hiding.

### CAREER SPOTLIGHT: **Dog Handler**

**Job Requirements:**

- K-9 training
- 30 days to bond with dog partner
- Military police

**Skills and Training:**

 Animal Care & Training

 Detection & Identification

 Law Enforcement

Explosive ordnance disposal specialists wear heavy armor called bomb suits to protect themselves from possible blasts.

A K-9 marine and handler

# TAKING CARE OF THEIR OWN

There are plenty of jobs in the U.S. Marines that support the soldiers behind the scenes. Legal services specialists are responsible for helping marine families understand military laws. These specialists also help families with the paperwork for wills, marriages, and divorces.

Food service specialists prepare food for soldiers. They plan healthy and balanced meals, playing an important role in making sure other marines get the energy they need to do their jobs.

CAREER SPOTLIGHT: **Legal Services Specialist**

**Job Requirements:**

- High school graduate or GED
- Type 35 words per minute
- Enlisted

**Skills and Training:**

 Legal Support

Preparing Documents

Communication & Research

# REACHING OUT

There are many marine jobs that are just like **civilian** ones. The U.S. Marines have their own police officers. Just like those in civilian life, military police officers direct traffic and prevent crime. They also provide security on bases. Marine band musicians play music at military ceremonies and official events.

Whether on active battlefields, on bases, or out in the community, the United States Marine Corps is full of soldiers with many important jobs. Together, they work hard to protect the country and its people.

★ ★ ★ ★ ★ ★ ★ ★ ★ ★ ★ ★ ★

The President's Own is a band made up of marine musicians. They play at the White House about 200 times each year.

# MORE ABOUT THE MARINE CORPS

## AT A GLANCE

**Founded:** November 10, 1775
**Membership:** Around 177,000
**Categories of ranks:** enlisted, warrant officer, and officer
**Largest base:** Marine Corps Air Ground Combat Center in Twentynine Palms, California

## DID YOU KNOW?

⭐ Non-marines can receive an honorary title in the marine corps. One member of this select group is a cartoon character—Bugs Bunny!

⭐ Marines in uniform are not allowed to put their hands in their pockets. This is so they look professional.

⭐ The marine corps mascot is a dog named Chesty. He reports to the Marine Corps Barracks in Washington, D.C.

Chesty

# ★ GEAR ★

**NIGHT VISION DEVICE**

**FIRST AID KIT**

**TACTICAL VEST**

**RIFLE**

**UNIFORM**

**RADIO**

**BOOTS**

# GLOSSARY

**ammunition** objects fired from weapons, such as bullets and arrows

**amphibious** relating to or adapted for both land and water

**analyze** to study or determine the nature and relationship of something

**civilian** a person who is not in the military

**combat** fighting or having to do with fighting between soldiers or armies

**enlisted** soldiers who have joined a branch of the armed forces without prior special training and hold a rank below officer

**explosive** a dangerous material that can catch fire and blow up

**infantry** the part of the military that fights on foot

**martial arts** style of fighting or self-defense

**missions** tasks that have a particular goal

**neutralize** to stop or make ineffective

**reconnaissance** a military activity where soldiers gather information about something

**recruit** a person who goes through the process of joining the marines

**simulated** made to look or feel real

**surveillance** a close watch kept over someone or something

**transcribe** to make a written copy of something

# READ MORE

**Conaghan, Bernard.** *Marine Corps (Serving with Honor).* New York: Crabtree Publishing, 2023.

**Coupé, Jessica.** *US Marine Corps (US Military).* Mendota Heights, MN: Apex Editions, 2023.

**Ventura, Marne.** *U.S. Marine Corps (U.S. Armed Forces).* Minneapolis: Kaleidoscope, 2023.

# LEARN MORE ONLINE

**1.** Go to **www.factsurfer.com** or scan the QR code below.

**2.** Enter "**Marine Jobs**" into the search box.

**3.** Click on the cover of this book to see a list of websites.

# INDEX

airborne and air delivery
  specialists 18
aircraft 18, 20
air traffic controllers 20
basic training 10
combat 8, 10, 12–14, 28
Crucible, the 10
cryptologic language
  analysts 4
dog handlers 22
explosive ordnance
  disposal specialists 22–23
fire team 14–15
legal services specialists 24

infantry 12, 14
martial arts 8
missions 4
musician 26–27
parachutes 16, 18
pilots 18, 20
police officers 22, 26
recruits 8–10
Revolutionary War 6–7
rifleman 12, 15
supplies 8, 18–19
vehicles 16–17

# ABOUT THE AUTHOR

Sloane Hughes lives on the Great Lakes, where she tries to be equal parts on land and in water. She has written numerous books for young readers.